I want to be a Pilot

Other titles in this series:

I want to be a Cowboy
I want to be a Firefighter

I WANT TO BE A

Pilot

FIREFLY BOOKS

A FIREFLY BOOK

Published by Firefly Books Ltd. 1999

First Printing

Library of Congress Cataloging-in-Publication Data is available.

Canadian Cataloguing in Publication Data

Main entry under title:

I want to be a pilot

ISBN 1-55209-449-9 (bound)
ISBN 1-55209-434-0 (pbk.)

1. Air pilots – Juvenile literature.   2. Aeronautics – Juvenile literature.

TL547.I25   1999   j629.13   C99-930931-5

Published in Canada in 1999 by
Firefly Books Ltd.
3680 Victoria Park Avenue
Willowdale, Ontario, Canada M2H 3K1

Published in the United States in 1999 by
Firefly Books (U.S.) Inc.
P.O. Box 1338, Ellicott Station
Buffalo, New York, USA 14205

Photo Credits
© Al Harvey, pages 5, 6, 7, 15, 18, 21, back cover
© Tony Cassanova, pages 10, 16, 17, 19, 22-23, 24, front cover
© Masterfile/John McGrail, pages 8-9
© Masterfile/Sherman Hines, page 14
© First Light/Brian Milne, page 11
© First Light/L. MacDougal, pages 12-13
© First Light, page 20

Design by Interrobang Graphic Design Inc.
Printed and bound in Canada by Kromar, Winnipeg, Manitoba

The Publisher acknowledges the financial support of the Government of Canada through the Book Publishing Industry Development Program for its publishing activities.

Some pilots fly small planes. This float plane ties up to a dock – just like a boat does.

Other pilots fly jumbo planes that take people to faraway places.

Large airplanes have many dials and gadgets in front of the pilots. One dial shows how fast the plane is flying.

Fighter planes like this one fly high above the clouds. Only very experienced pilots get to fly them.

When planes fly this high, there is not enough air to breathe. That's why the pilot wears a mask with a hose. The hose is connected to an air tank.

The best pilots are sometimes picked to fly at air shows. A group of planes is called a squadron. Air shows are thrilling to watch.

A pilot gets to see the world in interesting ways! This pilot can tell the earth is round.

Pilots carry equipment as well as people. The pilot of this helicopter is trained to put out forest fires.

Some helicopters are big enough to carry people long distances. This helicopter can land on water.

Fighter planes are used in the air force. They have only a small cabin. A pilot must lower himself or herself carefully down.

Every airport has a control tower. The people who work in the tower tell pilots when it is safe to take off and to land.

The navigator is part of the air crew. Navigators check the position of the plane in the sky.

It only seems like this pilot is in the sky. He's really on the ground – training to fly at night.

There are lots of things to check during a flight. Pilots use lists and keep careful records.

Some pilots feel like they are part of the plane. Can you see why?

It takes a lot of training to be a pilot but the hard work pays off. For a pilot, every new flight is a new adventure.